Notes of Forgiveness

Notes of Forgiveness

A Daughter's Journey and a Mother's Gift

Sarada Bonnett & Sandra E. Cordray

Strategic Book Publishing and Rights Co.

Strategic Book Publishing and Rights Co.
12620 FM 1960, Suite A4-507
Houston, TX 77065
www.sbpra.com

ISBN: 978-1-62857-444-9

This book is dedicated to:

All who find the courage to take what has happened in their life that caused them pain and create an opportunity of change; those who refuse to stay in the quicksand of excuses and self-pity, who choose to move forward and accept that life has handed them an opportunity to become great; and those who embrace the healing power of forgiveness.

I honor and applaud you!

Acknowledgments

I could not publish this book without saying thanks to the many people who helped me along the way.

To my mother, a woman of passion and talent, whose voice was a gift to all who heard her sing. Thank you for returning to me after death and leading me through the photos, news clippings, and memories to my discovery of you.

George Bonnett, my wonderful husband, thank you for being the man I can truly look to for support. I have such great respect for you and thank God every day that he gave me such a beautiful and wonderful gift.

Brandon, Payton, Madison, and Joshua without your love and support I would not have been able to take time to work on this project. You are the best children a mom could ever ask for. You have made me proud. Brandon, I pray that you are kept safe every day. I am so very proud of you and the wonderful man that you are. Payton, your love for animals, your drive, and your commitment to succeed are incredible gifts from God. You are as sweet and beautiful on the inside as you are on the outside. Thank you for making my day every single morning I get to see your smiling face. Madison, you have a calling in your life, my love. God has a very big plan for you. He has given you the ability to sing like an angel, speak to large crowds, and connect with people one on one. Use these gifts for his glory and you will be blessed. Josh, you are a wonderful addition to our family. You make me smile everyday with your humor and sweet demeanor. You all make my world a brighter place, and I am lucky to call you my children. I love you..

Sandy Cordray, this book would not exist at all if you had not come into my life. You are the most brilliant woman I know. I have the utmost respect for you. I stand in awe when I think of your accomplishments. You are so humble and loving. You are always putting others before yourself. I am so grateful that we are not only partners in this book project but also friends. God has truly blessed me. You are a true gift from heaven to all who know you.

Sabre Sabo, you are not only my best friend but also my sister. Your love and support over the past thirty-six years has made me a better person. I can't imagine my life without you. I have always said that you should give the world the gift of your story. I think you could help so many people through your trials and challenges. You have the strongest will of anyone I have ever met. I love you with all my heart, my beautiful sister.

There were so many people who helped me through many challenges in life, but I would be remiss if I did not say thank you to Shari Jasso, Connie Smith, Aunt Carol, and

Uncle Keno. All of you saw a need and filled it. I thank you for being the most unselfish people I know.

Gwen Plauches, Jessica Rapolo, Ryan Lowe, Brad Schroder, and Julie Andre: thank you for giving me the nudge that I needed, for the countless hours of listening to me, and for reading the first chapter more than once. I love you all very much and consider you more than a writers' group. You are my dear friends.

—Sarada Bonnett

For my husband, Carl Baribault, who always has faith in me.

—Sandra E. Cordray

Contents

Chapter 1   The Curtain Drawn   1

Chapter 2   What a Journey: Life in a Publicity
             Release   7

Chapter 3   What's in a Name?   17

Chapter 4   The King   23

Chapter 5   Singing with Buddy Holly and
             The Crickets   31

Chapter 6   Rockabilly Lives   41

             Gallery   49

Chapter 7   The Early Years   69

Chapter 8   Friends Become Sisters   77

Chapter 9   The Men in Our Lives   85

Chapter 10   My Life Changed Forever: Addiction   95

Chapter 11   Coming Full Circle   105

Chapter 12   Life Is in Session: Are You Present?   111

Chapter 13   Time to Go and Live   117

Chapter 14   Defining Moments   123

Epilogue   Faith and Forgiveness   131

ONE

The Curtain Drawn

To live in hearts we leave behind is not to die.

—Thomas Campbell

CHAPTER ONE

I remember standing in the cold, white, sterile hospital room where my mother lay on the hospital bed. She was covered by a white sheet and blanket. Tubes reached out from under the sheet, connecting her petite frame to monitors that emitted a whirring sound and intermittent beeps. This vibrant woman—my mother, who could command an audience of thousands when she sang onstage—was silent. For me, the silence was deafening.

Twenty-four hours before, I had been over four hundred miles away in Lafayette, Louisiana, singing the national anthem at the Louisiana Realtors Association installation of officers. I was having a grand time with colleagues, discussing the current market and listening to piano music softly playing throughout the meeting hall. The aroma from fresh flowers filled the room. A phone call I had missed from my stepdad, Hal, was the last thing on my mind, but after the third missed call I figured it might be serious. Still, I thought the call could wait because he was also my accountant. I figured that maybe he was calling about my finances.

I had no cause for alarm; everyone in the family was relatively healthy. The message Hal had left was to call him. It was midnight, so I decided to call him in the morning. Off to bed I went. The next morning started just like every other when I worked expos. I was running late to set up the display, but I'd done it so many times that it was second nature to me and not a worry. I hurried out of my hotel room, clutching a Styrofoam cup with hotel-brewed coffee in my hand.

Downstairs there was a maze of people mingling about the cavernous convention hall. Many appeared to share with me the signs of late-nighters. Others had a disheveled look that made them look as though they had forgone sleep.

It took me about forty minutes to set up the display. As I grabbed my briefcase, I realized I had left my cell phone upstairs in my hotel room. When I had a break at around noon, I rushed to my room to grab it.

Taking the elevator to my floor, I had a sinking feeling—the kind you get when you've just remembered something you were supposed to do but didn't. That was me as I stood there alone in the elevator, staring at each number that was illuminated as the elevator moved past a floor—that uneasy feeling in my stomach I couldn't even describe.

I called Hal back, and the phone call was brief. He used my pet name. "Surge, your mom is in the hospital, and I would like for you to come as soon as you can."

I told him my work would be finished in the morning, and I could drive directly to Dallas from Lafayette. He sounded hesitant but didn't disagree with me.

An hour later I got another call, this time from the hospital nurse. "Your dad didn't know how to tell you this, but we are basically keeping your mother alive until you get here."

I felt immobilized as the words echoed in my mind. My emotions took over, and I couldn't even speak. When I regained my voice, I told her I was on my way. I notified my colleagues that I would be leaving and that they could handle conference details without me. I wanted my children to be with me, so I called my husband and asked if he would come get me. In my state, I couldn't drive, and I needed my children.

The six-hour drive to Dallas seemed never-ending. I arrived at the hospital and found my mother in her room. As I approached her bed, I knew that time would not be forgiving—I could not will the minutes to become hours. I would not see my mother's deep blue eyes look back at me again. No smile would cross her mouth, and I would not hear her voice again. I could not fix this problem. I could not make her better. All I could do was to be there and witness the inevitable.

As my mom took her last breath, I felt as if a weight had been lifted off my shoulders. At the same time, however, there was an overwhelming sadness that enveloped me, as I felt that I had lost the chance to really get to know her—to understand who she was. My mom was gone.

At her funeral I felt numb. My mind was clouded in a fog of memories as I greeted and talked with the many people who knew my mother from a different time in her life. They all said such wonderful things about her, but I didn't really know how to respond. I thanked each of them, though, as their gifts of memory gave me comfort.

It wasn't until years later when the package arrived at my doorstep that I truly got a sense of who she was. There were boxes filled with photos of her that had been taken in Europe, Las Vegas, and Mexico—each one capturing a moment in my mom's life. As I looked at the pictures, I could see my mom smiling back at me from a time that had passed. I didn't know that within those boxes would be forgiveness, joy, laughter, and many cleansing tears. They opened a door for me through which I stepped into her life and came to rediscover her. And at the same time, I discovered who I was. Thus began my journey of forgiveness and healing.

TWO

What a Journey: Life in a Publicity Release

. . . best thing to come out of Texas since oil.

—Press release, 1956

CHAPTER TWO

My mom was born March 23, 1933, in Fort Worth, Texas. She was named Gwendolyn Joy Wilkinson, the thirteenth child welcomed by her parents, Walter J. and Della Wilkinson. Her father earned a modest salary working at Bluebonnet Packing Company in Fort Worth. Her introduction to music came at an early age, before she had started school, and she developed her singing technique while listening to Gene Autry records.

Mom's first job as a professional singer was for WBAP Radio in Fort Worth, singing with the Texaco Hired Hands from Burras Mills. By 1950, WBAP had started their first television station, which featured Bewley Barn Dance every Friday evening. When performing on the show, she was called Shirley Davis. Soon thereafter she also began singing for Burras's competitor, Bewley Mills, where she was given the name Sherry Davis. While performing on both shows, she believed that the producers did not fool the public into thinking she was two different performers, especially since her yodeling style was one of a kind.

There were more radio shows, and a few years later she traveled to California to take a job on *The Foreman Phillips Show* on KECA-TV in Los Angeles. Mom performed five shows each week, with a three-hour show on Sundays. Legendary singer and guitar player Merle Travis was also part of the show, and recording artist and radio host Tennessee Ernie Ford would sing bass on the show's closing gospel number. Other featured artists were Betsy Gay, Marilyn and Wesley Tuttle, Bill Sutton, Jack Tusker, Mary Lou, June Ray, Jimmy Widener, and Hank Colwell.

In a few years, Mom returned to Texas, where she was part of the *Gals of the Big "D" Jamboree* recordings (from performances in the 1950s at the Dallas Sportatorium). Among these singers were Helen Hall, Sunshine Ruby, the Lovett Singers, Betty Lou Lobb, and Charline Arthur. Mom had five songs on the record, most of which she barely remembered; however, she did remember working with Buddy Holly.

In a 2001 *Dallas Observer* article, Robert Wilonsky wrote about the Big "D" Jamboree of the mid-1950s, focusing on the female singers featured in recordings and the elusiveness of their stardom. The article quotes my mother:

"Buddy was crashing there at the little apartment in back of Norman Petty's studio, so when Norman Petty asked him and The Crickets if they'd mind backing me, they said no, they didn't mind. I didn't know it was Buddy Holly. I met him, and we all had a long conversation over dinner, so when he became famous, I realized this was the group that backed me. But my manager would not release 'Broken Promises' without the publishing rights, and none of the major record companies wanted to give us the publishing rights, because that's where they made their money. It was two years before my manager found a small company that agreed to let him have the publishing, and by then I had moved on and didn't have any interest in it whatsoever."

Shortly after recording with Holly, she did a Texas tour with Elvis Presley and then moved to Cocoa Beach, Florida. While she was there, she ran across John Glenn and a few of the Mercury astronauts and performed "Around the World" for them.

Recalling her singing years to reporter Wilonsky, my mom told him:

It would be very nice to know that people can hear the quality I worked so hard for—the study, the hard work. If they appreciate it, it would be great to know that, but I don't sing like that anymore, because I haven't sung like that in years. The voice is like any instrument: If you don't use it, you lose it. I will be excited if people get excited about it, but I don't know what I could do about it, except enjoy it and be grateful someone has done all this stuff. I can't believe those records were ever made at all.

For three years, Mom performed in Las Vegas at the Stardust Hotel as a lead singer in *The Sights and Sounds of Esquivel*. Juan Garcia Esquivel was a pianist, composer and arranger from

Mexico City who came to the United States in 1958 when offered a job by RCA Victor. His elaborately staged shows were part of the Vegas-Tahoe circuit. Vegas insiders and celebrities such as Frank Sinatra were regulars in the audience.

In one of Esquivel's shows, *Hello America*, Mom had numerous costume changes. She was ranked the nation's top yodeler, and Esquivel made sure his audience did not leave a show without hearing her remarkable yodeling.

Along the way her career was depicted by various newspapers, magazines, and radio personalities. My mother's publicity releases read like a compressed biography for a singer whom I knew through the eyes of a daughter, during a time when show business was a part of her past. As I read the release, I wondered how my mother responded to seeing the persona her manager and the publicity machine wanted the world to see in print.

Sherry Davis is the best thing to come out of Texas since oil. The sweet singing song bird has been a pro, since her teens. She was stage struck as a child and has since devoted her life and career to show business. Big things have happened to her, but she needs one more break to get to the big time where she rightfully belongs.

Sherry co-emceed a Fort Worth TV show, when TV was a new thing. She was a success of course, but her co-emcee got a better break. He is now the famous Pat Boone . . .

Naturally enough, in Texas, her first start began in country music, and while she can still out yodel many cowboys, pop music is her best field. Sherry starred for over a year on a Dallas TV program as a pop singer. She was also out in Hollywood, on TV, several years back as a country singer, appearing with Merle Travis, composer of "Sixteen Tons . . ."

Sherry has startling good looks and a natural style that bespeaks of talent. She is five foot two, has deep blue eyes, and beautiful jet black hair. The well-poised young lady does modeling on the side, between engagements, but show business is her business. Unmarried and in her early twenties, Sherry now books out of Dallas, TX, through Artists Services Bureau, the same office that handles the famed Sonny James and the rocking Gene Vincent.

In 1956, Mom starred in the Dallas *Opus '56* Sunday television show which also featured Earl Humphreys, Johnny Hicks, the Don Crawford Dancers, and the Sophisticates. As popular as this program was, the place for rockabilly was the Big "D" Jamboree, a radio barn dance in the Dallas area that showcased talented artists from 1948 to 1966. A poster for the Big "D" Jamboree show of October 27, 1956, reads, THE JAMBOREE'S SINGING SWEETHEART SHERRY DAVIS PERFORMS "LOVE ME TENDER." Months earlier, Elvis Presley had made the charts with the song. At the Dallas Sportatorium, the Big "D" Jamboree drew promising artists and also attracted Johnny Cash, Elvis Presley, Ferlin Husky, Carl Perkins, and many others.

In 2001, Dragon Street Records released the twenty-nine-track CD, *The Gals of the Big "D" Jamboree*. Mom sings "Chime Bells" and does her hallmark yodeling on the track. The record features my mom, as well as Helen Hall, Charline Arthur, Sunshine Ruby, the Lovett Singers, Betty Lou Lobb, Abbie Neal and the Ranch Girls, Doreen Freeman, Pat

Smith, Wanda Jackson, and Janis Martin. On this collection, Mom sings "Bop City," "Just A Little Bit," and "Broken Promises." "Broken Promises" is performed with Buddy Holly. Reviewing the album, Robert Wilonsky noted:

> In the end, what makes something like *The Gals of the Big "D" Jamboree* so intoxicating isn't just the music but the lost tales these women tell—of sharing stages with the likes of Johnny Cash and Johnny Horton, of playing with the Light Crust Doughboys, and of sacrificing their careers for their families. That, more than anything else, is why so many of these women have vanished from the history books. More often than not, they willingly settled down, had children, and left behind the hellish life of the touring bus. That's the very reason Sherry Davis gives for quitting show-business life in 1971—despite the fact she once recorded with Buddy Holly and The Crickets, toured Texas with Elvis Presley, and performed in Las Vegas for several years with Esquivel, whose music could, in the 1990s, become the soundtrack for would-be hipsters living in their space-age bachelor pads. [1]

One's life cannot be encapsulated in a publicity release. It is not measured in bookings on *The Lawrence Welk Show* when Mom replaced Alice Lon for two weeks at the Aragon Ballroom in California. Nor can it be judged when she performed for three years onstage at the Stardust Hotel in

---

1 "Girl Power: The Gals of the Big 'D' Jamboree Remain the Sweethearts of the Wrestling Ring," by Robert Wilonsky, *Dallas Observer*, March 3, 2001.

Las Vegas for the spectacular productions of Juan Garcia Esquivel. But as I researched my mother's career, I came to see how she was presented to her public, to her fans, and to the music industry through the filters of managers and show business. It was a choice she made because of her passion for singing and music. And through this view I also came to see how strong she was—enduring travel to the next engagement, living out of a hotel room, preparing for the opening of another show. And all the while, perhaps she was hoping for that big break that seemed to be just around the next corner. I read the first paragraph of the publicity release again:

Big things have happened to her, but she needs one more break to get to the big time where she rightfully belongs.

THREE

What's in a Name?

Through this I saw the glamorous side of Hollywood and knew for sure that I wanted to continue singing, and maybe someday I could taste that kind of success.

—Sherry Davis

CHAPTER THREE

Growing up, I never knew what to expect when the phone rang. Callers would ask for Sherry Davis, Della Lee, Shirley, and the list goes on. It was far from the normal greeting most of us get when we answer a call today.

Show business in the late '40s, '50s, and '60s was much different from the celebrity lifestyles we observe today. Managers and producers led the pack in control and earnings, and the talent was just that—the talent! Back then, most performers were motivated by their love of the music and would agree to almost anything if it meant they could pursue their passion for performing. My mom would change her name every time a new manager or sponsor came into the picture. She had many names, but there was only one that was near and dear to her heart. Tony Slaughter, a Las Vegas newspaper reporter, interviewed my mom during her stint as a performer in the city. Below are the contents of that interview:

Curtain Peeper Looks for Home Towner's

Las Vegas – Every time it's announced that a Fort Worth group is in the audience at the desert Inn's "Hello America" show, a petite Fort Worth girl breaks the house rules and peeps through the curtain to see if she recognizes people from her home town.

She is Della Lee, a featured singer in the spectacular show which has brought a congressional citation because of its patriotic theme. It's a show for the entire family.

People in Fort Worth wouldn't recognize her by her name. While singing and performing at WBAP-TV with Pat Boone in Fort Worth and the late Bobby Peters, the Bewley Barn Dance and the Texaco Hired Hands, she used the name of Sherri Davis. She also was Sherry Davis on a Texas tour with Elvis Presley.

And ex-students of old Handley High School wouldn't even recognize her by that name. She was born Gwendolyn Wilkinson, daughter of Mr. and Mrs. Walter J. Wilkinson, both now deceased and buried in Arlington. She had 12 brothers and sisters, six of whom are buried in Arlington.

In "Hello America" she has seven costume changes, coming on first as one of the Showboat Sextet in "New Orleans – 1880." She is ranked as the nation's top yodeler and does just that as an Indian Squaw in the show.

Her top role in the musical is a takeoff on Judy Garland in "Hooray for Hollywood," a skit from the "Wizard of Oz."

Before joining "Hello America" Miss Lee was a singer with Esquivel and his orchestra for three years at the Stardust Hotel.

She learned her singing technique in Fort Worth from Gene Autry records. And Autry, native of Tioga in Grayson County, later shed a lot of influence on the Fort Worth girl deciding on a show business career.

"It seemed that all of us, when we were growing up, loved and admired Gene Autry," she said, "but Bobby Lee, an older brother, idolized him. When we played cowboys and Indians, Bobby Lee always had to be Gene Autry. He always said that someday he would have a pair of boots just like Gene Autry wore."

"Since my father made a modest salary [Bluebonnet Packing Company] and had 13 to feed, mother would go downtown to Leonard Brothers to shop for groceries. There she could get better bargains and buy food in larger quantities," Miss Lee recalled.

One Saturday young Bobby Lee spotted a pair of wooden boots at Leonard's he wanted to buy for 98 cents to send to Autry. His mother explained that she didn't have the money.

"Besides," she said, "Gene gets so many gifts, he wouldn't even notice them."

Two days later Bobby Lee was sent home from school seriously ill. A piggy bank was placed by his bed and he told relatives and friends he was going to buy a pair of boots like Autry's. In five days the youth was dead.

Later the mother found the bank, which had 98 cents in it. She bought the wooden boots he had wanted to send to Autry and mailed them to the Hollywood star with an explanation.

Autry lost no time in thanking Mrs. Wilkinson and inviting the entire family to come to Hollywood as his guest.

Three years later the family accepted Autry's invitation and visited in his home. "We toured the grounds of his luxurious home and I took a swim in his pool," Miss Lee recalled.

"Through this I saw the glamorous side of Hollywood and knew for sure that I wanted to continue singing, and maybe someday I could taste that kind of success."

"Well I've continued and can say I earn a comfortable living but the glamour and excitement has turned out to be hours of hard work and study. Still, I wouldn't change it for any other line of work," she said.

And "Hello America," which is now in its second year, looks like it's going to be around for a long time, which means more hard work for Fort Worth's Della Lee, Sherry Davis and Gwendolyn Wilkinson.

And where did she get that last name of Lee? The answer is in the ninth paragraph from the top.

As I researched my mother's career, I realized that her name may have changed many times, but her talent and beauty remained the same. She attracted fans and admirers with her stunning looks and her perfect pitch. I can honestly say that, for the first time in my life, I felt proud of her and the strength she must have possessed to endure a life on the road.

She had many names to many people, but I just called her Mom.

FOUR

The King

Two roads diverged in a wood, and I—
I took the one less traveled by, and that has made all the
difference.

—Robert Frost

CHAPTER FOUR

My mother and Elvis Presley performed at the Big "D" Jamboree in Dallas, but their paths never crossed until Presley did his Texas Whirlwind tour from 1954 to 1958. Gordon Stoker and the Jordanaires was the backup band.

The Jordanaires met Elvis Presley in 1955 when the band was on *The Eddy Arnold Show* in Memphis. Elvis approached them and told them that if they ever got a recording contract with a major company, he wanted them to be his backup. In 1956 Elvis began having the Jordanaires on almost all his recording sessions. It was a relationship that lasted for fourteen years.

Mom's agent had landed a job for her as the opening act for Elvis Presley. I never learned how this happened, so I can only credit this to a savvy agent who knew that my mom had talent. Elvis's early appearances on the tour had low attendance; the performances were held at high school gyms and car dealerships. But that soon changed.

On October 11, 1956, at the Cotton Bowl and Texas State Fair in Dallas, Mom stepped onstage and faced twenty-six thousand screaming fans. They had come from all parts of the region and beyond to hear the King. She finished her last song, exiting the stage before a shower of coins rained down from the fans. This seemed to be the fans' way of showing their affection for the King.

The next evening's performance was in Waco. There were only five thousand fans to face that night, and as soon as she did her set, Mom retreated to the hotel. In less than twelve hours, she and the tour group would be on the road again, this time to Houston. But her plans for a quiet night were interrupted with banging on her hotel door. When she cracked open the door, three starstruck girls burst into the hotel room.

"Where is Elvis?" they demanded. They looked under the bed, opened the closet door, and checked the bathroom.

Mom told them he was not in her room. They did not believe her and searched again, but there was no evidence of anyone in the room except the four of them. They left with disappointment worn on their crestfallen faces. The scene repeated itself the following night in Houston, but Mom was able to secure the door and keep the uninvited guests out. This became a drill she perfected during the tour.

Mom had encountered fan after fan who just wanted to catch a glimpse of the King. However, none of them compared to the two girls she ran into outside of one of the venues. As Mom walked around before being called to makeup, she heard two girls sobbing. She had to find out what was going on, so she walked up and asked if she could help. The girls explained that they had sold all that they had to buy tickets and bus fare to the concert. The problem was that someone had stolen one of the girls' purses that contained their coveted tickets and tickets home. Mom grabbed the girls took them into the Coliseum with her. Not only did she give the girls bus fare home, but she also got them backstage to see the King up close and personal. Listening to the story as a child, I couldn't understand anyone selling what they had to go anywhere. Now I'm just in awe of the fans' level of commitment.

Traveling on the tour bus to a final show in San Antonio, Mom was asked by Col. Tom Parker's assistant, Tom Diskin, her thoughts about Elvis. Mom replied that he was a good performer, but she did not know him personally. Mr. Diskin seemed shocked that Mom could open for Presley without meeting the star. Mr. Diskin soon remedied that in San Antonio, arranging a meeting for the two a few months after they had begun touring together. There, during a press conference at Bexar Coliseum, Mr. Diskin introduced Mom to Elvis. She bore a strong resemblance to the actress Debra Paget, who had costarred with Elvis in the movie *Love Me Tender* (released November 21, 1956). There were reports that Elvis had a crush on the actress.[2]

The press conference continued. The press had taken their photos. Mom saw no need to stay, so she left. Later that day, Elvis paid her a visit, thanking her for being a part of the tour. The meeting was brief, and Mom ushered the King of Rock and Roll out of her room. She was not one of

---

2   *Elvis in Texas: The Undiscovered King*, by Lori Torrance with Stanley Oberst, Republic of Texas Press (2002).

those swooning, starstruck girls and had no desire to throw herself at him.

On August 16, 1977, I was six years old and living in Dallas. I can remember how much I loved to play Elvis Presley records on my record player. Whenever a new song came out by him, Mom made sure I had it. That August afternoon a friend phoned our house, notifying us that Elvis had died at the age of forty-two. Overwhelmed by grief, Mom sobbed for hours. Even as a young child, I could see how this loss broke her heart.

In 1999, Mom was interviewed by reporter Bryan Woolley as part of his series, "Where I Come From," a regular feature in the Sunday edition of the *Dallas Morning News*. The column was later turned into a book, featuring the interviews the journalist had collected over the course of a year. During the interview, Mom recalled meeting Elvis:

> "On the last night of tour, he thanked me for being on the tour with him and being the kind of person I was. He said, 'The guys tell me you're a Christian.' I said, 'Yes, I am.' I felt sure I was going to be put down for that, as I had many times before, but he said, 'Well, don't ever change. Because if it weren't for my faith, I wouldn't be where I am today.'" [3]

In the book's chapter about Mom, there is a photo of her dressed in one of her favorite suits. It features a matching striped collar and cuffs, along with a pillbox hat with a wide-striped band and striped flower. Mom holds a photo of her

---

3   *Where I Come From: As Told To Bryan Wooley*, by Bryan Wooley, University of North Texas Press (2003).

that was taken with Elvis when they were on the Texas tour. In the photo, she leans close to Elvis, her forehead touching the right side of his face. They looked like a match made for one another. No one knew how they read the Bible together after the road tour, nor did anyone know how they talked about their families and their love of music and singing. He respected her values and who she was. He was her favorite star. I believe that their faith was a unique and private bond they shared. Their faith and respect for one another translated into two people who worked together doing what they cherished—singing.

FIVE

Singing with Buddy Holly and The Crickets

Well, if she can also sing, that would be frosting on the cake.

—John Pickering

CHAPTER FIVE

When I was growing up, sitting around the kitchen table with my mom and her friends talking about the good old days was a frequent occurrence in my home. They would throw out names like Buddy Holly, Pat Boone, and Elvis Presley as if they were neighbors and friends. I was so unimpressed with all this chatter because I had no idea who these people were, with the exception of Elvis. When they talked about my mother's first demo record and the backing band, I didn't truly realize the significance of the conversation.

I connected with one of the backing musicians, John Pickering of the Picks. The Picks were John, his brother Bill, and Bob Lapham, their friend from their days at Texas Tech who sang baritone. One month before "That'll Be the Day" charted, Norman Petty and Buddy Holly asked the Picks to overdub Buddy's "Oh, Boy!" July 13, 1957, the

Picks overdubbed "Oh, Boy!" It soon became The Crickets' second hit. On October 12, 13 and 14, 1957, while Buddy and the instrumental Crickets were in San Diego and Fresno, California, the Picks returned to Petty's 7th Street Clovis Studio and overdubbed eight additional songs. Notable among these songs are "Maybe Baby" and "Tell Me How."

When I reached John by phone, he was full of memories of when he first met Mom for a recording. He said the day went something like this:

"We had no idea who we were going to record for. We would get a call from Bill that Norman wanted us over there to do some backup singing. So after we got off from work, we drove over there were met by two gentlemen and a lady who were there with Norman. She was introduced to us as Sherry Davis from the Big 'D' Jamboree. When we walked in to the session, we just weren't prepared for someone as beautiful as Sherry. We were in our twenties and so was she. 'Wow, who is this?' Bob Latham and I said to each other. 'Well if she can also sing, that would be frosting on the cake.'"

That day, the Picks had done several recording sessions. John said he could not remember much of them, but he does remember the one with Mom:

"We walked in and she was wearing a pink blouse and what looked like troubadour pants. They were white and they had lace-ups on either side of her hips—they looked like real long shoe strings that had been laced together and she just looked like a movie star, I am telling you. I don't know if you knew how beautiful she was. We were really excited about that. And then Buddy Holly came in with Jack Vaughn. Jack was the guitarist with the Norman Petty Trio, and that is where the Norman Jack label came from—Norman, Vie, and Jack, [who] were the original Norman Petty Trio. I think he wasn't playing with a group anymore. Norman called him in to play a duet with Buddy on the lead guitar backup. We were excited to see Buddy, and I've heard J. I. Allison also came and was the drummer, but I don't remember J. I. being there. And on the base I'm pretty sure it wasn't Joe B. It—it was Big George Edward. I am almost positive of that."

The Picks had never heard of Sherry Davis, but when she began to sing, they were mesmerized. In my phone conversation with John, he was not shy about sharing his enthusiasm:

"Oh, man, when she opened her mouth, we said, 'Gee whiz, all that beauty and that kind of a voice.' I tell you what, we were excited. We were around a lot of artists, but they were not like Sherry. They put her in the auxiliary studio, which was next to the main studio toward the door. We were set up in the large studio, where we could look right into her face. And the three of us were around one microphone. We didn't often use lead sheets because we would remember the songs—we felt like we could sing them better from memory. But in her case, we didn't need any more inspiration.

"I remember we took a break after 'Broken Promises,' and Bob told me, 'I think she likes me.'

I said, 'Oh! She's been smiling at me!'

"We actually had a little argument over which one she liked the best. Then it was probably Bill, my brother—the high tenor who was better-looking than either one of us. That was the effect she had on us, so we did our best singing. In fact, Bob is convinced it is the best singing the Picks ever did. And as far as listening to it, I agree with him. We devised our own back up. We did head arrangements—that is what we always did. We had no idea what the songs would be and we would come in, got through it a few times. She sang through it a few times with us and we devised what we wanted to do."

Later in our conversation, John recalled Buddy Holly's contribution to the sessions. "[Buddy Holly] had one of those large speakers facing off to the Picks. He set out on it, and Jack Vaughn pulled a chair up and they devised the guitar work that is on the song. He set up duet guitar lines—one playing the lead part and the other playing the tenor. On some sections Buddy was playing the riffs, and it was a magical moment."

Earlier that July, John and the Picks had recorded "Old Boy" with Buddy Holly in an additional session. When they returned for another recording, Buddy Holly told them how much he liked their singing. "He heard us at the Sherry Davis session. He and Norman asked us to do eight more songs, which we did in October. We did 'Maybe Baby' and seven other songs, and then 'Oh, Boy!' came out in November. Buddy never said anything to me about Sherry Davis and her voice, but I could tell he couldn't help but be impressed with her. I really wasn't paying any attention to him because there was a beauty in the house."

After their recording session with my mom, John learned that she was among the stars for the Big "D" Jamboree. "I figured she was going to be a big star, and that would have been a hit record—except it was before its time. Back in those days, country was 'real country.' Sherry could have sung anything, and she would have played over in the pop field. But they put it out on an independent label and nobody picked it up. They said it was 'too pop.'"

In 2001, the recordings by women who performed on the Big "D" Jamboree saw the light of day when David Dennard released the compilation album, *The Gals of the*

Big "D" Jamboree. My mom's voice is captured on the album, along with Helen Hall, Charline Arthur, Sunshine Ruby, the Lovett Singers, and Betty Lou Lobb. When I listen to their songs, I step back in time, trying to imagine that period in my mom's life.

I discovered similarities between John's career and Mom's. His parents began their career in music as the Pickering Family Singers. His brother Bill joined them in singing at age five. Six years later, five-year-old Joe joined, making them the Pickering Family Quartet. When John was seven, the family moved to Lubbock and then to Clovis, where he met Norman Petty, who was fourteen. For over twenty years John and Norman sang professionally, performing on the stage, in daily radio shows, and wherever else their fans took them.

John never saw Mom again after the recording session in Clovis. He had heard about her opening gig for Elvis Presley and Frank Sinatra. He believes that success was difficult for female singers of that era, and it was challenging for both female and male artists to break away from the hold of managers. Country music was dominated by men, and beautiful women who tried to show their vocal talent did so in an industry that valued beauty first and vocals second.

John shared with me his thoughts about the challenges of the business. "You had to perform in places filled with drunks and under a cloud of cigarette smoke. If you did a four-hour gig for dances and the like, your eyes would swell shut by the time you finished from the thick tobacco smoke. I hoped that [Sherry] went on and did a lot of stage work and that sort of thing, because [touring] wasn't any place for a real lady."

When I told John about her career in Las Vegas and assured him that her career was not spent in smoky dancehalls, he was thrilled. "That's super," he said. "She should have been in Las Vegas. She could sing, as far as I'm concerned, as well or better than a lot of them. She reminded me of Patsy Cline—her voice wasn't as low, but she had a timbre to her voice that could have made her very successful. I am glad to hear that she went on and had some success."

As for The Crickets, their adventures in show business were plagued by pitfalls of their own, mirroring Mom's challenges in many ways. John shared with me: "We had about a twelve-year hiatus because people weren't told that we were the voices of The Crickets, which didn't help our careers since the instrumental Crickets got credit for all of it despite lip-synching. Nobody had even heard of the Picks. For twelve years, we went to Nashville as the Pickering Brothers in country music after a layoff of twelve years. Eventually, we got a contract with Stomp Records, releasing two or three hit records as the Pickering Brothers. 'Proud Mary'"and a version of 'Words' were on their way toward helping us make it big. Unfortunately, the record company went bankrupt."

John's break came with the arrival of the Internet, which he used successfully to promote the Picks' back catalogue. During his stint recording at Clovis, the band's management told John and his bandmates that the studio was spreading the word that the Picks did the vocals. It was not until 1981 that John went to the Buddy Holly Memorial Society convention in Lubbock, Texas, and fans were able to meet the voices on "Old Boy" and "Maybe Baby." The vocal group for The Crickets won best vocal group of 1957 in both the United States and the United Kingdom. Until then, John had not known that it should have been the Picks who won those awards.

If Buddy Holly had not died in the plane crash on February 3, 1959, the story of John's career may have been different. As a result of his efforts, John called MCA in 1984, requesting more songs for re-recording. He and the Picks overdubbed them and distributed them across Europe to a responsive audience.

John told me that the music industry did not care if the talent was male or female; everyone was at the mercy of their managers. He and his fellow singers never received any monetary compensation for The Crickets' Buddy Holly recordings. Rather, their work was done in exchange for the promise of publicity that would enhance the group's visibility.

"We were told it would help boost our popularity because of our relationship with Buddy Holly, who already had 'That'll Be the Day' out. We did 'Oh, Boy!' and then in November of 1957 *The 'Chirping' Crickets* album was released. What listeners didn't know was that we are on nine of the twelve songs. They didn't mention us anywhere. In fact, they implied that The Crickets did their own singing. We got nothing. We even didn't get paid for the sessions. The total for all the trips I made, some of them were almost fourteen hundred miles round trip from Corpus Christi to Clovis and back for a weekend . . . for all the times we went over to Clovis I ended up with sixty-five dollars for expenses. For the next twelve years, I called Norman and told him. He told me, 'Oh, me and the boys, we are telling everybody about it. They know what you've done.'"

But in actuality they didn't. In 1981, fans were excited when they met John and the other band members who were the actual voices of The Crickets. It was after this meeting that John decided to do something about the error. After spending his time, money, and effort, he persuaded MCA to send to him more Buddy Holly solos for overdub, as he had done for "Oh, Boy!" and "Maybe Baby." The Picks added their voices a week to ten days after their solo sessions. John then released the new recordings on his own label, selling enough copies to break even on the endeavor. He then contacted MCA once more, leading the company to send him even more masters for overdubbing that are now for sale online.

When Charlie Records in England heard about the newly completed retakes, the company licensed them from John for sales overseas. Today, the albums, featuring Buddy Holly and the Picks, have worldwide distribution. What's more, in 1990 the Picks finally made their first dollar as a result of these efforts. Before the remasters, John and the group never made any money from singing with The Crickets.

When I asked him why he pursued this for over 40 years, he said "It kept me alive. When you've got something worth sharing, you figure you've got to do it—you just live and do it."

I told him he had the passion and purpose my mom did. "You bet," he replied.

SIX

Rockabilly Lives

If I'm going to use my voice to influence people . . . I might as well influence women to be at least stronger and more powerful. I think that is what your Sherry was doing too.

–Kim Lenz

CHAPTER SIX

Bop it to the left, bop it to the right
Bop it down the middle and you hold your baby tight
Then you go, go to Bop City
Go, go
Go to Bop City

—"Bop City," Sherry Davis

Nearly fifty years after Mom recorded "Bop City," I can listen to it on the CD of *The Gals of the Big "D" Jamboree*. After finding the record widely available online, I was fortunate enough to connect with Kim Lenz, a Los Angeles–based rockabilly musician and singer who spoke with me about my mom's legacy, the influence rockabilly has had on contemporary musicians, and how the challenges of the music industry today mirror those of the past.

It was Dragon Street Records, the label for which Mom recorded, that brought Sherry Davis to Kim's attention. During a visit to Dallas, the producer showed Kim the warehouse that was once the home of the Big "D" Jamboree. He also shared with her an old track that had been released in 1996. On it was Mom's recording of "Bop City."

Speaking to me from her home in Los Angeles, Kim shared her thoughts on my mom's musical history: "[Dennard] had all of these great photos of your mom, and I was very intrigued by her. She seemed like such a woman ahead of her time. He said I should do this song, and I said, 'Oh, why not? It sounds great.' So we recorded 'Bop City,' released a forty-five, and after its release I signed a record deal with High Tone Records. They only printed about five hundred [copies] of the forty-five, making them kind of a collector's item now. Later on, I made a full record with High Tone and started touring a lot. During my shows, I did 'Bop City' for quite a few years. I am thinking of reviving that song because I now have harmony singers in my band. My bandmates and I talked often about Sherry Davis. I don't know that much about her—just the information I was told and the pictures I was shown."

Kim told me that Mom's performance of the song initially attracted her to the track. "That time period was kind of magical in country and western music," she told me. "She was trying to bring in rhythm and blues beats, and she was obviously one of the very early people to have done that. She brought in a little bit of pop sensibility to what she was doing too. It is such a fun song. I liked her delivery and thought, 'Let's do it.' I think it was her delivery that made me want to do the song."

When recalling her first exposure to the idea of being a musician, Kim recalled hanging out in the '90s-era music scenes on the West Coast, never thinking that she would become a musician. But at the age of twenty-five she did just that, albeit accidentally.

"I started jamming, made a forty-five with 'Bop City' on it, and the next thing I know, I have a little record deal with High Tone, which was the best record label for rockabilly at the time."

For Kim, rockabilly is rock and roll at its purest. "Rockabilly is the beginning of rock and roll and is very passionate music to me," she said. "When I listen to Sherry Davis and others during that period that passion was there as well. It was a magical period. To be historically correct, rock and roll was around in the African-American community as early as the forties, but their lead instrument wasn't guitar. Their lead instrument was usually a saxophone or a piano. The magical period began when both blacks and whites started making rock and roll by mixing in contemporary local music. In Memphis this created rockabilly."

Kim continued, "For the first time, different cultures started hearing each other's music, putting all their good ideas together. It must have been such an exciting time to be a performer. We take this for granted today. Even when I first found out about Sherry Davis, the Internet was still a new concept, and music like hers was typically discovered through word of mouth. You would have had to find out from a person like David Dennard or through books."

Kim told me she felt that my mom was from a time that must have been magical because it helped create rock and roll as we know it today. She said it was like the Big Bang, when everything came together.

"Rockabilly has a universal appeal, I think, because it is the base of everything that we listen to now. It's the root from which everything else came—call it 'roots music.' Roots music encompasses hillbilly, rhythm and blues, and all the great American art forms of music. I consider rockabilly to be a great American art form of music."

Kim's band, the Jaguars, is a cosmopolitan rockabilly outfit with a guitar player from Barcelona, a drummer from Dallas, and a bass player from St. Louis. The band released four albums total: one in 1998, another in 1999, a compilation album in 2005, and, after a few quiet years, the band came back in 2010 with its latest album. Just as Mom's record went over well in England, Kim says people love rockabilly across the Atlantic as well.

In addition to original songs, Kim likes to include covers of popular and obscure rockabilly hits from the genre's heyday. Doing so, she feels, keeps the legacy of strong women in music intact. "I like to pay tribute to the great stuff that has been recorded to help people remember. I am always playing with words and phrases, and my overall inspiration comes from being a woman in a culture and time where we still have to be tough and stand up for ourselves. Many of my songs come from that perspective." She continues, "I think the songs [act as] a good role model for other women. If I am going to use my voice to influence people, or if people are going to listen to my music and be at least slightly influenced by it, I might as well influence women to be stronger and more powerful. I think that is what your mother was doing too."

Kim's favorite song on her 2010 album, *It's All True!*, is "Rambling Feeling." She wrote the song because, historically, country music and rockabilly music involve men writing songs about how they have to leave. They are rambling men, but the women always want to keep them. In Kim's song, however, this dynamic is changed: the woman leaves a man who begs her to stay.

"I wrote 'Rambling Feeling' from a female perspective that says, 'You're really great, but I have got to get out of here.' I like to put a different spin on things, showing that a woman can escape the paradigm that she was presented with. It's shocking to me that we are still caught up with a lot of the same issues we were dealing with in the fifties. While we do have a lot more freedom as women now, I think we still have to stand up for ourselves."

So from a song that Mom recorded in the '50s to now, I have been provided with one of life's moments where the past comes full circle. When I hear Kim tell me about what music means to her, I see my mom sharing the same beliefs. Both women were blessed with talent and loved rockabilly.

Kim told me, "Music is still part of the fabric of our lives, and I feel it is a privilege and a responsibility to be a musician. You can make something that people listen to that makes them feel something. That is what all art is about. The world that we live in, the mundane, everyday world we live in, can feel kind of dead. We are all looking for meaning, looking to feel something. That is why we have art, photography and the visual arts, film, and TV. We can feel happiness, sadness, joy, or a range of other emotions. Our ability to experience emotions makes us feel alive. For me, music accomplishes this better than any other art form. I think that music can be healing. It is a privilege and a responsibility for me to write music that will be fun for listeners and also add something to their life; give them something."

I think of Mom and how she did just that. I believe that every time she stepped onstage to perform or to sing to an audience of one—i.e., her daughter—she felt alive.

Gallery

A picture is worth a thousand words and a million memories.

Gwendolyn Joy Wilkinson, 1930s

Gwendolyn Joy Wilkinson singing for war bonds, 1930s

Gwendolyn and Gene Autry's wife, Ina Mae. This is where it all truly began for Mom. . . .

One of Mom's first gigs—still innocent, still bright-eyed and
ready for the world

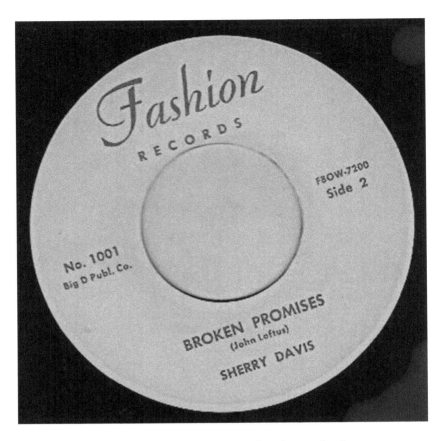

First record with Buddy Holly playing backup

My mom was so excited that they released this CD, even though she really couldn't sing anymore, because of her advanced age. It just meant so much to her . . .

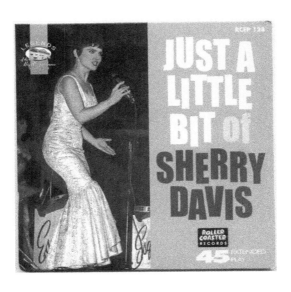

I was so excited that this came out before she passed away. She worked so hard and was truly one of the best in the business.

This is one of my very favorites. When Mom would show me this picture, you could see a sparkle in her eye as she remembered opening up for the King. What a memory.

Mom took this candid shot while walking back to her dressing room. I remember saying, "Mom, that was Elvis Presley!" She would reply, "And I am Sherry Davis!" I had to love her confidence.

Hello America in Las Vegas

More pictures from *Hello America*

My favorite movie as a child was *The Wizard of Oz*. When my
mom pulled out this picture, it took her about an hour to
explain to me that she was not the girl in the movie. This was
one of the skits from *Hello America*.

Another favorite of mine. She was so angelic and
peaceful in this picture.

Isn't it funny how pictures and music can give you instant recall of times past? My mom would pull out this picture and say, "Now, Sarada, this is how you want people to take your picture. Shooting up at this exact angle will make you look taller and slimmer!"

Pat Boone and Mom. (I'm not sure what her stage name was at this time.) I would be so embarrassed if I ever met this man. My mom told the producer of the radio station on which she was working live shows that Pat was handsome but couldn't sing worth a lick. Ummm, Mom, that was Pat Boone!

Who taught my mother how to use the microphone? Sammy Davis Jr., that's who! She was such a humble person and always looked to her costars for advice. She told me that not only did he work with her onstage, but afterward he would always give her tips on this or that. What a great guy.

One of the first pictures I had taken with my mom. I was only a few weeks old.

SEVEN

The Early Years

"He who sings scares away his woes."

–Miguel de Cervantes, Don Quixote

CHAPTER SEVEN

At a very early age, my mother was told that she wouldn't be able to have children. Being a mother was the one thing she had always dreamed of as part of her future.

She was in California working at the Sands Hotel when her dream of motherhood came true. Imagine the surprise she must have experienced when her doctor told her that her next costume fitting might need to be let out! She told me that this was the best feeling she had ever experienced. I have early childhood memories of Mom stroking my hair, kissing my forehead, and telling me that being in front of thousands of screaming fans could not replace the feelings she experienced when she became a mom.

My mother was amazing. As a young child, I remember her putting together plays and puppet shows to entertain our family. We always had a house full of children, of all ages, visiting and playing. She had such a big heart and always wanted to help others.

At the same time, she was very keen on teaching me the lessons of the Bible, and she would walk around the house quoting scripture to me. If I disobeyed her, she found scripture. Her favorite was Proverbs 22:15: "Foolishness is bound in the heart of a child; but the rod of correction shall drive it far from him." If I was sassy, there was scripture for that too. Her favorite was Exodus 20:12: "Honor thy father and thy mother: that thy days may be long upon the land which the Lord thy God giveth thee." She had scripture for just about every situation. I am so grateful for this; the very thing that used to drive me insane keeps me sane now. There is something invaluable about being able to recall scripture in a time of need. I don't know if that was my mother's intent, but for me it was a gift.

My early childhood years were okay for my mom and me; she had enough money saved to take care of our family for a while in Irvine, California. Because she had done very well in show business, she could afford to stay home with me for the first few of years of my life. When I was about four, Mom got a call from one of her brothers, my Uncle Charlie. He was feeling ill and asked if we could come to Quinlan, Texas, to help him with his nursery. My mom was the youngest of thirteen children, and the wide span of years between her and her oldest siblings made her the baby of the family. I had heard a lot about Uncle Charlie. My mother adored him and would do anything for him.

Being the sweet woman she was, Mom agreed and we made our way to Texas. We lived with Uncle Charlie for one year, helping with his multi-acre nursery while he returned to good health. I learned much about my mother during that time. She had such a caring and giving spirit. She was a hard worker and an amazing caretaker. She always put others, including me, before herself. If I wanted it, she found a way to provide it—even if she had to go without.

She loved her brother deeply, and it broke her heart when the time came for us to leave. As hard as it was to leave, though, she felt that she could not support us in Quinlan; we needed to move closer to Dallas. Our funds had run out and it was time to face reality.

She liked to say, "No, Toto, we are not in Kansas anymore." She said this often during these years. I would laugh at this, never really knowing exactly what she meant. Now I know what she meant, and I use the same saying with my children.

We didn't quite make it to Dallas and settled instead in Mesquite, about twenty miles from the city. It was an interesting place that would prove to have a profound influence on my life. I learned many life lessons there and met many people who would change the way I viewed the world.

Of the many memories I have from Mesquite, I recall vividly our first night in our new apartment. We had no furniture—not even a mattress. We had given up everything to move to Texas, leaving everything but our clothes behind in California. That night, Mom lay on the floor next to me. She was crying, though she didn't know that I was awake. She and I were so close, both physically and emotionally, that I knew when something wasn't right.

I slept snuggled under my mom's chin. For me it was the safest place on the planet. For some reason that night, she had not been herself and I could tell that something was seriously wrong. When I felt her tears on my forehead, I knew for certain that something had upset her. I asked her what was wrong, and in the most courageous voice she could muster, she said, "Baby, Mommy wants the best for you, and I feel I have made so many mistakes. Maybe we shouldn't have left your Uncle Charlie. You had a warm bed to sleep in and a table where you could eat your food. We have nothing."

Years later, these memories still bring me to tears. As a mother myself, I empathize with the pain she was feeling and the uncertainty she experienced while taking care of her young daughter. When I heard her say this, I said to her, "I would rather be in our own place, right where we are, than any other place in the world. Mommy, we have each other."

She laughed, cried, and went on to tell the story many times over the years. Only now do I realize how much of an impact that evening had on her and me.

Soon afterward, she started answering phones for a company in an office park. After answering calls for six months, other tenants in the building asked if she was willing to answer their phones too. She had a lasting impression on the companies she worked for, and her voice served her well in her newfound position.

Her salary at the office park was not fantastic, so she started selling Jafra makeup on the side. Because she had been a stage performer for well over twenty years, she had a knack for applying makeup that made this work a great fit for her. I learned my first lessons in sales as I tagged along with her at her Jafra "parties" on weekends. Though she called them parties, the young and naive me called them boring. I did, however, learn valuable sales and marketing skills, along with the proper techniques for applying makeup. These were all very helpful tools (although if you had asked me then, I would have told you otherwise).

In addition to this work, Mom would sing and wait tables at a local piano bar. When I asked why she worked so much, she didn't miss her chance to provide me with scriptural reasoning. This time, she quoted Proverbs 12:24: "The hand of the diligent will rule, but the lazy man will be put to forced labor." This scripture always stuck with me because, as a witty child, I would always respond to that by saying, "What kind of labor is this if not forced, Mommy?"

At least she would laugh and not scold me too badly.

EIGHT

Friends Become Sisters

Friends are relatives you make for yourself.

—Eustache Deschamps

CHAPTER EIGHT

My mother and I were extremely close. She always made me feel safe and secure. Although she worked many jobs, I knew she was always there for me. There was nothing I felt I couldn't accomplish knowing that she was in my corner. I was the only child—and a very selfish, spoiled one at that. It was not in a bratty way, but more in the "I'm the center of attention" kind of way.

When I was very young, my mother instilled in me respect for others. When she gave up her life in California to take care of my Uncle Charlie, she taught by example compassion and accepting others unconditionally. We didn't have much, but she always found a way to help others with what we had. She had such a beautiful heart.

I guess that's why my mother flipped a gasket when she found out that one of my schoolmates, Sabre, was walking home from school alone. Now, this was in the '70s, when children could ride their bikes and play outside unattended. However, a five-year-old walking home was a bit extreme even back then.

Sabre and I had met in class. We hit it off and immediately became best friends. At recess we made a sport out of chasing little boys around what we called the "big H," a solid concrete structure that looked like an H. It was used as a handball court.

There were two boys we thought were the cutest boys we had ever seen. One was quiet but funny, with reddish-brown hair and freckles. The other boy was loud and had only one front tooth. They bore the brunt of our mischievous little game. We chased them and told them we were going to kick them where it hurt if they didn't kiss us. The funny part is that we are all still friends to this day.

One day Sabre asked if I could walk home with her. I told her I would ask my mom when I got home. I was sure that it wouldn't be a problem. When I made it home that night, I asked my mom if I could walk home with Sabre the next day. You would have thought that the world was coming to an end. My mom exclaimed, "What?? A five-year-old walks home from school alone?!"

I didn't think anything was wrong with this picture, so I sat looking at her wide-eyed as she explained that something could happen to Sabre. She saw that tears were welling up in my eyes at the idea that something could happen to my new friend. She assured me, "Baby, tomorrow Mommy will drive you both to her house and talk to her mom. Maybe she just needs a little help." Again, Mom with the big heart. Years later, I don't have to wonder where I got my constant need to help others.

The next afternoon, Sabre and I climbed into my mom's lemon-yellow Pontiac and headed to Sabre's house. My mom expected to find Sabre's mom there but instead found a dark, empty house. I could see that my mom's blood pressure was rising; she always became a bit rosy in the cheeks when she was mad, and it was not from her Jafra makeup. She would also become a bit short-tempered and start calling me "Sarada," emphasizing each syllable.

Sabre's mom did not make it home until after dark that night. As we sat waiting, Sabre took us around the house. As we walked through this immaculately kept home, my mom asked questions about what Sabre usually did when she got home. Sabre spouted off a chore list that would scare any normal person, but it did not intimidate this five-year-old little girl. Sabre was so mature and handled herself so well. To me, she did not seem to be a child at all. But she was a bit scared when my mother explained that we were not going to leave her until her mother got home.

When her mother, Sandy, finally arrived, she gave Sabre a look, and it wasn't a welcoming "I missed you today" kind of look. It was a "What the hell are these people doing in our house?" kind of look. Sabre explained that my mother had given her a ride home from school and wanted to meet her mom. My mom politely asked to speak to Sandy in private.

We will never know what my mom and Sandy said behind closed doors, but I can only imagine that my mother was very matter-of-fact about a child being left home alone and the consequences that would follow.

After my mom and Sandy returned, Sabre got to come home and spend the night with me. All was well! Although Sabre and I never knew the arrangement made between our mothers, what we did know was that Sabre spent so much time with us that my mother looked at her as her own.

We were Mom's little princesses. If we wanted to do drill team, then we did drill team. If we wanted to take dance, then we could take dance. We would discover that there was a slight difference between our home and the homes of other children: we had a dance floor built in our family room so that my mother could listen to make sure we were doing the correct steps. Yes, she would *listen* to see if we were doing the correct steps. The woman had incredible hearing. It was as if she had sonar capabilities. I could practice while she was cooking in the kitchen, and she would yell out to me as I practiced, "You missed a step. Do it again." And she was always right!

This came in handy when it was time for tryouts. There was not a year that went by that Sabre and I were not captain or co-captain of our squads or that we didn't get the lead in a dance recital or play. We were my mother's life. She didn't date or have any social life until we were almost nine. My mom didn't want to bring different men in and out of our lives, and for that I am grateful.

There was a dark side to our arrangement with Sabre. Just when things finally started feeling normal, Sandy would come back into the picture. Each time Sabre would leave our home and go back to her mother, she returned to us different. It was almost as if a bit of her innocence was gone. The light in her eyes would dim, and she and I would have to work at bonding again. Don't get me wrong—we were extremely close, but it was almost as if she was mad at me.

Eventually, I found out all that she endured each time she would return to her mother. She was raped and emotionally abused, and I couldn't stop it or speak of it. She begged me not to tell because she loved her mother, even though she allowed this to happen. I promised Sabre that I would stay silent. This only made our bond stronger as young adults; no one knew her secrets or mine.

When I started to write this chapter about my mom and our early years with Sabre, I asked Sabre if I could include this information. Sabre agreed to let me talk about her abuse, but would not let me talk about who abused her.

The last time I remember Sabre living with us was in the sixth grade, right before we moved to Quinlan. I had no idea I would miss her so much. We had both grown accustomed to always having each other's back, and when she wasn't around I felt a hole in my life that nothing could fill. She had truly become my sister. My mom had started drinking and retreating into her own world, and as much as I would miss Sabre, it became necessary for us to move.

NINE

The Men in Our Lives

Any man can be a father. It takes someone special to be a dad.

—Author unknown

CHAPTER NINE

My biological father left us when I was two, leaving my mother to raise me on her own. There were men, however, who made an impact on my life as well as my mother's. There was Hal Leakey, who married my mom when I was nine. I think he gave her the stable home she had longed for and desperately needed. He taught me that I didn't have to be his biological daughter in order for him to love me unconditionally. That was such a big deal for me at that time in my life.

My Uncle John was my mother's favorite brother because he always took care of her growing up. That's why she was there for him when he needed her. He taught me many things when I was a child, some of which I will never forget, including patriotism and the importance of loving this country. He lived his life as an act of dedication and gave of himself without expectation of anything in return.

Dr. W. A. Criswell taught me practical life lessons regarding my faith and how to pray. I loved him and had the utmost respect for him.

Zig Ziglar touched my life in a very unusual way, as he did for thousands throughout his career. To this day, his voice rings in my ear, saying, "That's just stinking thinking!" or "See you at the TOP!" He gave me an attitude adjustment many times.

I only bring these men up because I feel so blessed to have had their guidance in my life. I hope that every young woman who doesn't have her father has some strong male figure in their life who can make a difference.

My mom met Hal Leakey when I was nine. They hadn't been dating for long when, all of a sudden, they were married. As a matter of fact, I have no recollection of them dating at all. Up until this point, the only man in my life was Uncle John, who came to live with us to help raise me and, later, Sabre.

John was an amazing person who had lived a very interesting life. He was a World War II veteran and had told stories about things he'd seen that would make the hair on the back of my neck stand on end. Most of the stories were about barroom fights and what it was like to be away from home. He made them very G-rated, of course. He was the one who taught me how to play poker and, most important, how to keep a poker face—a skill that has proven useful in negotiations ever since. Uncle John would cook for us, and he basically raised me. Whenever I left the living room a mess, I remember hearing him say, "Sarada, go in your room and grab another toy. There is a spot in the corner you forgot to decorate." That was code for, "Get in here and clean up your mess, young lady."

Sabre and I gave him so much grief. For example, Sabre once decided to try an amazing stunt on her bike, which had what we referred to as the "infamous banana seat." Her plan was to jump over a hole in the ground, which she said she had tried before and had cleared safely. That was the story I got after the fact. Trusting Sabre and believing she had more wisdom than me, I hopped on the bike with her. I think I should have asked what the plan was before agreeing to get on the back of the bike. I'm not sure which one of us at that point was the idiot.

She rode around our swimming pool, building up speed, when—*wham!*—she unexpectedly hit a hole. The impact punctured the tire, sending me five feet in the air. Meanwhile, Sabre headed face-first on the concrete. Uncle John could do nothing but watch his niece fly across his window as her friend screamed, blood streaming down her face. The event was traumatic for Uncle John, and I'm not convinced he ever truly recovered from the fright that we gave him.

Hal, on the other hand, was a mild-tempered accountant who was so far off the radar from what I was accustomed to that I didn't how to take him. Hal, who had a dry since of humor, was a soft-spoken, mild-mannered gentleman. He would open the doors for me, pull my chair out, and stand when I left the table. There was only one thing wrong with him in my eyes: He slept with my mother. I had slept with my mother for nine years, and this new arrangement turned me into Satan's incarnate. I would sit at their bedroom door at night and yell, "I hate you! I hate you! I hate you!" I would sob and kick and scream. I could hear him tell my mother, "Let me take care of her." The first time this happened, I thought I was done for as he opened the bedroom door to approach me. Hal was six foot two—a big man; I was the smallest child in my class. But he just came from the bedroom, scooped me up, and took me to my room to put me in my new bed, which he and Mom had bought to soften the blow of sleeping in my own room.

His efforts didn't really make a difference to me, even though he would sit beside my bed, hold my hand, and pray with me. He would tell me that he was not trying to take my place, but that he was trying to be a part of our family. I would look up at him, as he was being so sweet to me, and say, "Then you sleep in here, and I'll sleep with my mommy!"

The other important men in my life came to me through church.

At age five, I discovered the wonderment of Children's Church. Early on Sunday mornings, my mom would put me on the bus headed to Mesquite's Calvary Hill Baptist Church. Every week, I would look forward to Sunday morning. It was the highlight of my week. As the bus drove away each Sunday, Mom would wave to me. Working three jobs during the week left her too exhausted to go to church, but she always made sure her daughter got on the bus.

When Hal and my mother married, we returned to the First Baptist Church in downtown Dallas, my mother's church before she moved to Las Vegas. At our new church, my pastor played a major role in both our lives. Dr. W. A. Criswell, in my eyes, was the epitome of perfection. He started his career at the church in October 1944, serving for fifty years as senior pastor, preaching over five thousand sermons from the pulpit.

He published fifty-four books and was awarded eight honorary doctorates. The Criswell College, First Baptist Academy, and KCBI Radio were started under his leadership. Additionally, he served on the board of trustees of Baylor

University, Baylor Health Care System, Dallas Baptist University, and The Baptist Standard. Dr. Criswell had come to First Baptist Dallas, and he remained there as pastor until his death in 2002.

I will never forget the first time I met Dr. Criswell. Mom had built him up so much to me that, at that first meeting, I put him in line with God. After service, he greeted our family and welcomed Mom back to the church. They talked about what she had done after leaving home and about her career as an entertainer. Here was a church with over ten thousand members, and he still made time for each of his parishioners.

Knowing that he was there for our family meant the world to me. He handed me his phone number and said, "Sarada, if you ever need anything, call me." And I did call him. I phoned his office and told the secretary that I needed to speak with my pastor. She giggled and asked what this was in reference to; I told her it was private. She said that she could make an appointment for me.

I needed to see Dr. Criswell because I had begun having issues with Mom. She had become more of an alcoholic. I confided in my stepdad that I needed to see our pastor. Dad knew what was going on at home, but it was the big elephant in the room that he would not talk about. He worked long hours to support our family because my mom no longer worked. He just didn't have the time to deal with her alcoholism, as he was worried about paying bills and maintaining order in the family. As a result, he dealt with the problem by ignoring it. When I told him I wanted to talk to Dr. Criswell, he told me he thought it was a good idea. I told my mom I wanted to see my pastor. She was thrilled, of course.

Looking back at that time in my life, I see now that I was on the brink of realizing I wasn't a child anymore. I felt that my mom's addiction robbed me of my childhood. Most children of alcoholic or drug-addicted parents will say the same thing. I was no longer a child at that point, and I felt that I was no longer safe—and up until that point I had felt very safe and secure. I had been a princess my entire life. Whenever I wanted something, it was there for me. But now I realized I was alone. There was no protection.

As I waited outside Dr. Criswell's office, I felt nervous. I wasn't sure how I was going to tell him why I wanted to meet with him. I followed his secretary as she opened his office door and announced my arrival. His office was a handsome and stately room, and at its core was Dr. Criswell, sitting behind his immaculate desk. I wish I could include a picture of this man. He reminded me of a jolly Santa Claus, but without the beard. I sat down in a big chair facing his desk. I was still a child, so my feet dangled above the floor. My hands were folded in my lap. In my eyes he was perfect. When he spoke, I immediately felt better, as if someone was watching out for me and that he was my protector.

"How are you, Sarada?" he asked me.

"I need prayer," I told him.

He started laughing. "You need prayer?"

"Yes, sir, I do."

I began telling him about the situation at home: about how I didn't feel stable anymore, how I felt like I was losing control at school because I didn't want to go home. School was my safe haven—the closer it got to the dismissal bell, the antsier I became. It took great effort for me to focus because I felt trepidation and did not want to go home. Eventually, some of my teachers picked up on this and called in my parents for meetings—that is, when my mom could sober up enough to attend. When she did, she painted a completely different picture of our home life to my teachers.

I shared all of this with Dr. Criswell. He put his hands together and told me, "You know you have someone to watch over you every day. It's not me, but I talk to Him, and I will talk to Him for you."

His words made my spirit soar. As I left his office, I knew I was very safe because he was talking to God for me. I had a peaceful feeling talking with Dr. Criswell. I felt like I could always call his office and get some kind of answer. I believe that God gave him to me. He was a gift. I trusted him and felt an instant bond with him. He was the father that I never had.

I don't think my visit was very long, but it seemed long to me at the time, as my parents were waiting outside for me. I kept thinking that the longer I was in there, the more trouble I was going to get into. What if they asked me why I was in there? I had no idea what I would say. These thoughts were in the back of my mind, but it was imperative that I tell my pastor what was happening. I believed that if I just told him about the problems I was facing at home, he could fix them. He was my lifeline as I struggled to keep my family intact. I was becoming angry at God because I did everything I could to tell Him I needed help, but I received none. I had begun to feel forsaken until this meeting.

Dr. Criswell told me that he was going to pray for me and my family, and that he and members of the church family would watch over me. They did their best to include my parents in church functions and always asked me over for dinner. This helped, but there was nothing anyone could do without addressing the problem head-on. My mother so good at putting up the facade that our world was perfect that everyone knew what was going on but didn't know how to help without her cooperation.

Why is this important? Dr. Criswell was one of the only stable men in my life until Hal, and he remained so until I moved to Louisiana. Dr. Criswell was an amazing man of God, and I was blessed.

This brings me to the next man who had an impact on me—someone whom I had never met. That man was Zig Ziglar. Mr. Ziglar used to teach my parents' Sunday school, and I would often sneak in to listen to his lectures. I had read all of his books and was drawn to his upbeat attitude.

From a very early age I knew I wanted to be in sales. So it was only natural that I would sneak in just to hear Zig Ziglar teach. Hal would get irritated with me because I would read Mr. Ziglar's books and picked up some of his expressions. I had a fondness for "See you at the top" or "That's just stinkin' thinkin'." I think Hal's tolerance was tested when he would express displeasure about something I had done, and I would respond that he needed a "check up from the neck up!" That was not well received by Hal.

It was Mr. Ziglar's teachings however, that gave me the attitude adjustment I needed whenever anything bad happened in my life. I learned from him that life is what you make it and that in every bad situation you must find the positive. Life is too short to focus on what you can't change, so learn, grow, and make a positive impact on the world around you. I believe he was a true gift from God.

TEN

My Life Changed Forever: Addiction

We must embrace pain and burn it as fuel for our journey.

—Kenji Miyazawa

CHAPTER TEN

When I was a kid, I always welcomed any opportunity to compete, and I loved to skate. My mom would take me on Friday nights to a rink in Mesquite called Broadway Skateland. I was a natural, I think, from all the drill team and dance lessons from my childhood. Ron Davis, the owner of the rink, had a son, Ronnie. Ronnie competed in dance skating competitions between neighboring rinks. One night, Ronnie and I started skating together. I guess we caught his dad's attention, because he asked me if I would be interested in partnering up with Ronnie for duo competitions. We could compete, but we would have to practice every day. My parents thought it would be good for me because it was something I enjoyed. The caveat was that we had to move back to Quinlan. Ron owned several rinks, but their home was in the country, and the rink where Ronnie spent most of his time was in Quinlan. How ironic that we would move to the very place my mom had left to help us get ahead. This was when my life changed forever.

Moving back to Quinlan meant leaving Sabre and the world I had found to be perfect for so long. Sabre would have to move back with her mom, Sandy, who would not allow her to move with us. This meant that I would not have the security of knowing that Sabre was okay.

My mom had started drinking at the beginning of my sixth-grade year and had become very depressed. I thought that moving might help her find some happiness by reconnecting with a familiar town. Maybe a fresh start would get her out of her funk. It was a tough call for me. I was worried about Sabre but even more worried about my mom.

The move was great. I made lots of new friends, and our house backed up directly to the school. I thought this was a very convenient setup for having friends over. My mom was feeling better and was very busy decorating the house and getting me involved in pep club and beauty pageants.

Things seemed to be back to normal for about a month. Then she slowly started regressing to her sullen, secluded mood. I would come home and find her locked in her room, smoking it up with a cigarette between her fingers and a glass of vodka in the other hand.

This became the norm, and I became more defiant. I had a tendency to say things I was thinking without thinking it through, the kind of things you wish you could take back because you know you're going to get in lots of trouble as soon as the words have left your mouth. One day I came home from school, and my mom asked me about homework—as if she ever paid attention to my work or to me. I just snapped and said, "Like you care. You don't care about anything but your drinking and smoking. What happened to you? Why are you such a waste of space? Who do you think you are, asking me what's going on at school?"

I slammed her door and went to my room. A few hours later, she came into my room. She was somewhat sober and told me she was sorry. I asked her why she was the way she was. She explained that she would never blame me for giving up her life as a singer, but that she missed it deep in her soul. She missed being onstage, doing what she loved every day, making people happy with her music, pleasing the crowd with her perfect pitch—she loved that. She said singing brought her joy, just as I had when I was younger. It hurt to hear her say this, but I'm sure that, in her mind, it was okay to say things like that to her pubescent daughter. The attention she received, the ability to have a plan and something to work toward, and living her passion were vitally important to her. She said that I was her passion, but I had become my own person and didn't need her anymore.

It wasn't until much later in life that I realized exactly what she had given up. I would hear stories from some of the greats, like Sammy Davis Jr. or Cyd Charisse, about my mom and how she was able to meet interesting people. But I had no idea what her life was like before I came into the picture, nor did I show an interest in her singing career, which must have been hard for her. Anything that she wanted me to do, I rebelled against; if she "suggested" that I sing in a play, I would stop and not sing for a long time, or I took things to the extreme, such as my weight. I became anorexic. Our relationship changed: she became angry, and I became defiant. She became increasingly critical of me, as well; if I got my hair done, it wasn't blonde enough for her. If I dieted, I didn't lose enough weight. If I sang at school, I was flat. If I was on the homecoming court, I had to win. When she would drink heavily, she would become complacent. I found solace in her alcoholic absence.

I would come home from school and find her on the floor passed out in her own vomit. I would pick her up, put her to bed, and clean up the mess. She had become addicted to prescription pills, including meprobamate, one of the medications prescribed when she was diagnosed with Parkinson's disease. Her favorite mixture was four times the recommended dose and a vodka chaser.

I would get upset with her because I couldn't have friends over to our house. She would stumble out of her room, mumbling to herself, and I couldn't stand being there. It got to the point where I didn't want to be at home at all. I wanted to die. I felt as though no one understood me. There was not a safe place for me anywhere. At school I felt like I didn't belong because no one really knew me. They only knew the perfect picture I painted for them. I was pretty isolated from other family members because my mom lost touch with them when she lost touch with the world. I was truly sad and alone.

It was at this point that I began to cut myself—not for the attention, but because I truly wanted to die. Some people say that if you really want to die, you will just find a way to do it. Well, I found a way several times. I didn't tell anyone. I didn't talk about it. I just did it. Every time, Hal found me just in time. When I would wake up in the hospital, I would be upset because I knew I had to go back home.

Funny, that word—home. For me, it didn't feel like a home. For Hal, I imagine it was a place of incredible stress. While he was dealing with my mother's mess, I tossed to him another mess. My life became more about my mom and her addiction than about just being a preteen. My mom retreated from the world, becoming fearful of public places. Our home was her safe haven, and as a result of her growing isolation and anxiety about the outdoors, she was diagnosed with agoraphobia. If Mom had to leave the house, she would limit where she would go and avoided open spaces. As a result, there was no chance of her ever going to a shopping mall, a restaurant, or anywhere with many people. She feared having a panic attack in public and not being able to stop it. A woman who had traveled the world and performed onstage in front of thousands of fans was now overcome with anxiety at the thought of being in public.

As a result of her mounting problems, I felt I was no longer the child. Instead, I became the mother. I felt that I needed to be the one who took care of Mom. As a result, I became angry. I was angry at her, angry at God, and angry at myself. I felt that the situation at home was somehow my fault. As I grew older, I tried to forgive many aspects of my mother's behavior that had upset me during this time. It has taken many years, lots of prayer, and therapy just to get to the point where I can see all the good that my mom did—and all the hell she endured in her lifetime.

I longed for my mom to be normal. I wanted to have dinner at my home, seated with my family. I wanted her to scold me when I did something wrong. I craved predictability in my life. Living in a home affected by substance abuse, however, does not yield itself to predictability. For many years I did not believe my own perceptions. My mother's addictions were the thieves that robbed me of my childhood.

I felt I wasn't good enough anymore. I went from being the light of Mom's life to being the one who caused her pain. She got worse, much worse. One day I found her lying on the floor in a pool of blood. At this point in my life, I thought I had become numb to anything pertaining to my mom, like the time I found her passed out in her own puke or found her cursing uncontrollably at the TV. "These stars today have no idea about talent, hard work, and dedication!" she ranted between gulps of vodka.

But that day was different. She wasn't breathing. At that moment I felt helpless. A sick feeling came over me; I just wanted to curl up in a fetal position and cry. This was odd for me because, up until this point, I was the mom and she was the child. When I walked in to find her almost dead, I didn't know what to do. I called Hal and then dialed 911. I felt like an emotional hurricane—fear and panic coursed through me like a storm surge at full speed, followed by the quiet calm that keeps one on edge as the rest of the storm looms. I felt a rush of adrenaline, which kept me from collapsing in fear, followed by intense anger, upset with her that she had done this to herself. When EMS arrived at our home, I was overwhelmed with fear as I watched the paramedics work on her. I remembered overhearing them say, "This doesn't look good."

At the hospital doctors periodically visited Hal and me in the waiting room. They expressed their concerns about Mom's condition. When they left, I would talk to my father, becoming cold and angry again. As you know, my life truly changed when we moved to back to Quinlan when I was almost twelve. At that point life had not been the same, but this was when my life changed forever.

This time she had taken it too far. Hal and I decided that she could not be alone. He asked me if I would consider homeschool so that I could watch her, taking care of her as best I could in case this happened again. I loved him—he worked so hard, and I felt this was the least I could do for him. Unfortunately for me, this meant giving up the only solace I had: being out of that house and away from her.

Homeschool was a bit tricky because I would be the one responsible for my own work. However, I didn't want to fall behind just in case this new situation didn't work out. These were the days of paper and pen, not computers, so my dad would always check my work when he got home.

Life was not at all what I had envisioned, and I felt disillusioned by what I was experiencing. I remember having to write a paper for school about my home life and how I felt about being homeschooled. I titled the paper "Baby Sitter" and filled it details about what the day was like for me. At 9:00 a.m. there were English lessons and checking on Mom, who was still sleeping. At 10:00 a.m. was math and another check-in on Mom, now in her room smoking. At 11:00 a.m. was social Studies and feeding Mom. Noon was break time and usually conversation time with Mom. The topic would be how the music industry has changed, and she had no problem telling me that she felt there was no talent in the business.

This report did not go over very well with my dad, and I had to write another one. Due to my mother's fluctuating condition, family outings were always fun during this period. We went as a family only to church because it was the one place my dad could get my mom—the alcoholic, drug-addicted agoraphobe—to go. On church days I tried to rise early and get ready so I had enough time to help Mom. By 9:00 a.m. she would have usually downed a few pills and would be opening a bottle of vodka. To be helpful, I would apply her makeup to make sure she didn't leave the house looking like we were going to take her to a Ronald McDonald look-alike contest. Once we arrived at church, our next challenge was negotiating our seating so that my friends or their parents wouldn't try to talk to her. I would always have to stop and use the bathroom to time our entrance into church just as the choir started. I feigned sickness as my strategy for our early departure from church. After services, we would usually get breakfast from a drive-through on our way home.

Once, however, my mom was adamant that we stop at an IHOP near the church. Fear came over me as she picked up her Dr Pepper can, her disguise for straight vodka. After taking a swig, she said, "SSARRRADA, we are going to the IHOP!"

I thought, *Great, I can see how this is going to work out for me!* As we were seated, my friends from church came into the restaurant, one by one. Every time the door opened, my heart sank. Halfway through our meal, my mom said she needed to go to the bathroom. I asked her if I could walk with her, knowing she would knock something—or someone—over. She replied by slamming her hands down on the table loudly and slurring, "I think I can go to the bathroom on my own!"

My eyes were as big as saucers as my dad reassured me, "Shug, she will be fine. Just follow her." So I let her go. Sure enough, her hand missed the table, caught the side of a coffee cup, and spilled the coffee everywhere. She reached the bathroom while I was cleaning the spill.

I remember hearing a very loud thud and scream: "SARADA!!" By now everyone in the restaurant was quiet. I felt everyone was staring at me as I smiled graciously and nodded as if to say, "I know I'm in hell right now." Some people put their heads down, a sign of empathy for my situation. Such is life.

ELEVEN

Coming Full Circle

Then your light shall break forth like the morning, your healing shall spring forth speedily, and your righteousness shall go before you; the glory of the LORD shall be your rear guard.

—Isaiah 58:7

CHAPTER ELEVEN

It's a funny thing about family. They are supposed to make you feel loved and secure. That wasn't the case for me when it came to my biological father, who had left me wondering why I wasn't wanted. The way one is raised as a child has much to do with his or her predisposed idea of self-worth. It wasn't until I was in my thirties that I came to understand how a person I had never met could have such an impact on my life. He was my biological father, Kenneth Gilliland.

My mother and Kenneth divorced when I was two, leaving me with no memory of him. I always wondered what kind of person could just leave his child. As I grew older, I felt sorry for him and wanted to find him, but I feared that he would reject me again. My curiosity prevailed over fear, though, and I tried at least three times to find him. I had no success in my searches.

When Hal and my mother married, they had to advertise in every US newspaper to notify my father that Hal was going to adopt me. When my mother told me they were required to submit this notification, there was no response from Kenneth, leaving me feeling rejected all over again.

In October 2008, I put out one last feeler just to see what might happen. I got a lead in the form of an e-mail from a woman who was helping me. She had found an obituary and believed it to be Kenneth's. Upon receiving this news, I felt my heart grow heavy: Part of me was glad to have an end to the journey, but the other part of me felt cheated because I would never obtain answers to my questions. Questions like: *What happened with my mom? Why didn't you want me? What is our medical history?* As I received the news in my quiet office, I opened the files that had been sent to me. I read that he was survived by his daughters, Nancy and Linda, who lived in Kansas. I wanted desperately to get in touch with them, but I didn't know what to say. Should I just call and say, "Hey, I'm your sister, and I'll send you my birth certificate to prove it. I just wanted you to know I was out here." Or maybe I would tell them, "Hey, did you know my dad? Oh, he was your dad, too?"

I sat crying for hours on my office floor because I was so excited to find out that I had sisters. The thought never crossed my mind that they might not want to know about their father's other daughter. I called a friend for advice.

"Are you thinking this through, Sarada? What if they don't believe you? What if they already know about you, but they didn't want to find you?"

Her questions made me nervous. I felt that I was on a runaway bus and had to get off. I had never entertained such thoughts. I consoled myself by saying that they needed to know I existed.

"If I were in their shoes," I said, "wouldn't I want to know?"

I obtained a phone number for Nancy. As I dialed the number, I felt nervous and excited. After waiting on the line, an answering machine picked up the call and I left her a message. After I finished, I wondered if leaving a message was an unwise idea. Two hours later, my phone rang. Like me, Nancy worked in real estate, which made me wonder if we had crossed paths at any point without realizing our potential relationship. The Nancy I had called, however, was not the half-sister I was searching for. We still had a great conversation and a laugh. Apparently I had given her quite a scare. She did tell me, though, that there was another Nancy with the same last name in Olathe, Kansas, and it was not the first time she had been contacted by mistake.

Encouraged by this call to try again, I called the new number in hopes of finding my sister. An answering machine picked up this time as well, so I left a message. Shortly thereafter, my phone rang again, but this time my half-sister was on the other end talking to me. Tears flowed when she told me our father talked about me all the time and how he wanted to find me one day. I asked about her family and also asked why my biological father had not responded to the adoption announcement. As Nancy went through her history, I came to realize that he had been in jail during the time! I was in shock. I had formulated countless scenarios explaining why my father never responded to the newspaper notices. I entertained thoughts that he was still in the military. Maybe he was overseas and couldn't get home. Maybe he was even a spy for the government, but he looked at my picture every day, just wanting to get home to his baby girl. I had a great imagination as a child, but I never imagined that he was in jail for robbing a bank.

Despite our enlightening and emotional conversation, closure was still forthcoming. It took me about a week to process all the information, but my heart didn't feel empty anymore. I also began to realize that I had a family about whom I knew nothing. For the next month, I was like a faucet, spewing questions about Nancy and Linda's family. When my excitement died down, I yearned to know more about Kenneth. I would have loved the chance to lay eyes on him, just once, even if it was through bars. I needed the closure.

As a result of this yearning, I discovered a program at my church facilitated by Jan Stevens called "One Day with God." The camp allows children of incarcerated parents to come together, spending the day learning about God through crafts. I believed I had found my calling, giving both the inmates and their children time to heal. As a volunteer I had the opportunity to mentor and assist children and their fathers as they had lunch, made crafts, and prayed together. This was such an emotional experience for me, more so than I would have expected. Watching the fathers reach out to their children and their children embracing them with pure and nonjudgmental eyes was such a blessing. As I interacted with them, I felt such a release, as if saying to my biological father, "It's okay. I understand that you were human and imperfect, and I forgive you." Sitting at the same table, making small talk and sharing a meal, even if it was just burgers and chips, was nothing short of a blessing for these incarcerated men. For one day fathers and their children were together, reunited by a unique effort called Forgiven Ministry.

TWELVE

Life Is in Session: Are You Present?

Above all, be true to yourself, and if you cannot put your heart in it, take yourself out of it.

—Anonymous

CHAPTER TWELVE

I always felt that I was present in my life but, at the same time, compelled to control my world and the world around me. This survival instinct came early as I tried to correct the imbalance in my family life, as well as the imbalances resulting from my mother's unhealthy choices to smoke and drink.

Though the Bible tells us to honor our fathers and mothers, I did not do this growing up. If I could go back in time, this is among many things I would do differently. I cannot do this, though, so I try to honor my mother's memory by making a difference in others' lives through volunteer work and by reaching out to provide the support I used to carry my family through rough waters. I am thirty-eight years old, and it took thirty-seven years for me to realize how much my mother gave up and what that meant for me.

I can't help but think that if she had continued singing and doing what she loved—what she was passionate about—I would have been able to witness the wonderful gifts of singing and performing that my mother had been given. Instead of celebrating my mother's talents and putting her on a pedestal, I hid her from my friends, my life, and my memory.

In my attempts to bring a sense of normalcy into my family's life, I covered for her when she was drinking. I hated the smell of smoke on my clothes. I took pride in how I took care of myself. My friends could smell smoke on my clothes, but I told them I did not smoke—never explaining that my mother was responsible for the smell on my clothes. I would have to go to school, shower in the gym, and change clothes. I used to tell my friends that our washing machine was broken and ask if I could do a load at their houses. I would wash my clothes, fold them, and put them in my locker so I could change at school. Because I was on the track team and cheerleading squad, I could enter the school early, shower, and change clothes before class. My day started before everyone else's just so I could feel normal and avoid the stigma of being a smoker when I was not one. As difficult as this was to juggle, it was how I survived.

Throughout my life I have always had many balls up in the air at once, but this is how I have survived for so long. Even before my mom passed, I felt like I was not accomplishing anything if I was not busy. My mother was an agoraphobe who sat in her room all day, drank, smoked, read the Bible, and watched TV. Sometimes she would write letters to TV personalities, giving them advice on how to improve their work. This was the extent of her activities. I would try to tell her she had to do something, whether it was to try new things or volunteer. She couldn't, and I didn't understand why. I didn't understand her Parkinson's, and I didn't understand her agoraphobia. All I wondered was how such an amazing woman could be stuck in her room, not attempting to live.

She and I did not reconcile until after she passed away. I feel that in her heart she truly wanted to be the best mom she could be, but she gave all that she could give. As a mother myself, I realize I am the woman I am now because of the way she raised me. These experiences are the things that God gave me. It was a gift, albeit in a distorted way. I realized this after my mom died, and I was able to forgive her.

Each of us has that right, that possibility, to invent ourselves daily. If a person does not invent herself, she will be invented. So, to be bodacious enough to invent ourselves is wise.

—Maya Angelou

I believe we are given a gift at birth; that gift is God's will in our lives. Find God's gift and build upon it. Wake up each day with purpose. For some, that purpose is to be a stay-at-home mom. If that is the case, be the best one there. Teach your children how to garden, work in a mission, tithe, or engage in other spiritually and mentally engaging activities. Give your children something to be proud of by setting an example.

For other people, their purpose is their careers. The same logic applies: find a personal passion and follow it through the grace and strength of God. I watched my mom turn from an amazing and vibrant woman into a miserable, lost woman. Now, as I reflect on her life, I begin to understand her through those who knew her and those who followed her career. I believe that she lost her purpose. I don't fault her. I wish I had recognized it earlier so that I could have helped.

If you wake up every day and wonder, "Is this it? Is this all there is?" then soul-searching is necessary. It is crucial to find out what makes you happy because not knowing turns this question into a self-fulfilling prophecy. One Sunday, my pastor spoke about God being a "big God." I believe that. I believe anything you feel He is calling you to do is possible.

If you were to ask your neighbors what makes them happy, most would probably say it is something other than what they are doing professionally. Why is this so? Most will tell you it's because of the demands of getting by and that "life happens." Taken from another perspective, life is what we make of it—and it is shorter than anyone realizes. God wants the best for all of us. I believe He wants a life driven by interest and talent instead of by mere obligations. God wants us to live happy and fulfilled lives, not directionless lives in which we forfeit our dreams. Answer this for me: do you think that God would call you to do something if He was not willing to give you the tools necessary to complete? The saying "Life is God's gift to you, and what you do with that life is your gift to God" should not be taken lightly.

Look at other people. What qualities do you admire in them? When you look at others, what gives you an uneasy feeling or makes you question who they really are? To recognize these qualities, good and bad, in others, you must possess them yourself. Take a closer look at your life and see whether or not there is room for improvement. By doing so, you can forgive not only those who may have hurt you, but also yourself for not following your dreams.

THIRTEEN

Time to Go and Live

A life without cause is a life without effect.

—Barbarella

CHAPTER THIRTEEN

My mom was truly an amazing woman, and despite her talent and compassion, I saw firsthand what caused her pain and eventually took her life. She stopped doing what she loved and lost her passion and purpose in life as a result. If someone does not know what his or her passions and purpose are, there can be great solace in prayer.

I can only equate the love that God has for His children to the love I have for my own. When I think of my mother and all the gifts she was given and passed on to me, her greatest gift was love. God sees us as His children regardless of our circumstances. I know that my mother had many faults, but not one of those faults was so bad that God would turn His back on her. I can only imagine that each time she fell and turned to alcohol, God was there to give her a hand back up. As I have come to terms with our sometimes strained relationship, I try to emulate this compassion by forgiving her for the hurt I experienced while she went through her own struggles.

In modern society, it is sometimes hard to remember that life is not about money, fame, or climbing up the corporate ladder. Ultimately, life is about love. Our greatest commandment in the Bible is from Matthew 22:37–39: "You must love the Lord your God with all your heart, all your soul, and all your mind."

Look at the people who have made a difference in this world. First and foremost is Jesus Christ, who lived every day with perfect love. Mother Teresa said, "It is not how much we do, but how much love we put in the doing. It is not how much we give, but how much love we put in the giving." Archbishop Desmond Tutu said, "Good is stronger than evil; love is stronger than hate; light is stronger than darkness; life is stronger than death. Victory is ours, through him who loves us." All these people made a phenomenal impact on our world. The thread that linked them was their knowledge that "the greatest of these is love" (1 Corinthians 13:13).

Who forgives all your iniquities, who heals all your diseases.

—Psalms 103:3

In the above passage, it is apparent that God will deliver us and heal both our earthly and spiritual aliments. My mom was an alcoholic for most of my life, but if you asked me today, I would tell you my most memorable life moment was when she had me in her arms, showering me with her warmth and unconditional love. I would also tell you that it was when she would pinch my arm because I was talking too loudly in church. These memories show her love and guidance despite her illnesses. She provided me with love and also the guidance of a strong Christian upbringing. That was God's work. He didn't turn His back on her, nor did He ever turn his back on me.

Anyone who has experienced what I have experienced sees the work of the one healer, Christ Jesus. I cannot express enough the importance of praying for God's guidance as I do every day. It can help calm the mind, hone one's focus, and provide perspective during challenging times.

FOURTEEN

Defining Moments

There is a defining moment in every person's life. Within that moment, everything that that person is shines its brightest.

—Anonymous

CHAPTER FOURTEEN

E very one of us will have a defining moment that creates an opportunity for change and growth. The question is, are we in too big of a rush to realize when that moment has arrived? If we do realize it, do we take time to reflect and learn how this moment could test, shape, and possibly change the course of our lives?

I have had more than one defining moment and missed the boat on a few. Some were more positive than others, but each had a great impact all the same. One such moment made me realize that we are not always fully aware of the power of our words and actions, and the impact they can have on others.

My first defining moment came when I was ten years old. It was a moment when I felt the sting of words that my mother could not take back. We were at our house in Mesquite, Texas, sitting around the dinner table. Sabre and I sat across from each other, my dad sat next to me, and Mom was at the head of the table. Sabre and I were talking about what we planned to wear that night to the skating rink.

My mom looked at Sabre and said, "Well, you know Sabre is a natural beauty." Then she turned to me and said, "You have to work at it."

Her words stung me. I looked at my dad and saw his eyes well up with tears. He looked at Mom and told her firmly, "You will never say that again." Then he hugged me and he said, "You are beautiful, baby."

My mom said nothing. I think she realized what she had said, but she could not take back the words. They had been spoken.

I will never forget that moment. I can even recall what we were eating. I remember looking down at my tuna croquette and peas, thinking I had to work at my looks. And from that point forward, I did. I worked out in the gym until all hours. I didn't eat much because I wanted to be thin. My hair was bleached blonde. That was the year I made captain of the drill team. From then on, everything was a competition for me. I decided to show everyone how good I was when given a challenge.

But in my mom's eyes, whatever I did never seemed to be enough. Life became a competition for me, and it remains so to this day. I won Professional Business Woman of the Year in 2010, which was given by Professional Business Women of St Tammany. I was Rookie of the Year in 1999, an award given by St. Tammany Association of Realtors. Now that I look back on these awards, they do not evoke a positive emotion; instead, they reflect an addiction to success and the accolades that follow. In the end, I thought I was seeking my mother's affirmation, but I was only seeking approval from myself. I had to have goals, and I had to meet them.

I can trace this behavior back to that moment at the dinner table. It is a memory I will never forget. This defining moment was when my relationship with my mother changed and, in doing so, changed my outlook on the world.

The second defining moment for me came in the form of a letter from my mother. As I read the letter, I realized that she had been the best mother she could possibly be given the tools she had available. The letter was dated December 26, 1998. In it, she wrote to me about her career and recently rediscovered recordings:

> It's hard to explain these tapes because until recently, I didn't know that they still existed. I don't think I listed "Humble Heart," which was recorded at the same time as "Broken Promises." I did that session in Clovis, New Mexico, in the Norman Petty Studios. Buddy Holly and The Crickets backed me on guitar and vocals.
>
> The others were recorded from my radio shows. You know about the four songs that were done in Las Vegas with the orchestra from the Sands Hotel and the one "La Malagueña" with Esquivel.
>
> The last two, "God Speaks" and "Did You Stop to Pray This Morning," were done at the American Music Corporation in Hollywood in 1953. They are old and have been played so often that they are scratchy, but I wanted you to have them. Unless more turn up, these are all I have.
>
> Tell Brandon that Grandma in Texas sends her love with "Little Boys." I hope he will always love it and remember me.

Sarada, I'm thankful that you remember the things I taught. I only wish I had been a better mother and taught you more. If I had only been a better example for you and Sabre, maybe I could have spared you some heartache.

Another blessing is [your husband] Roy, and that you love and respect him. Pray for each other and your precious children as I, too, will pray for all of you.

Love each day seeking God's will because He put you here for a purpose. Be patient and He will lead you.

My mom embraced this belief. She had enough faith to take God's hand and believe that He put her here for a purpose. I believe that purpose was of many forms and shapes. Singing was her passion. It gave her purpose and direction and led her to many opportunities, including touring from Texas to California—and the world—three times. Along the way, she performed with many talented people who shared her passion for music. Additionally, God led her to become my mother. Before I was born, she shared her voice on the world stage. When I arrived, her stage was my world—and I was her audience. I had her in my life for almost the same amount of time that she pursued her singing career. God put her here for a purpose. God led her to be my mother, and I was blessed.

My third defining moment came to me through my children. It taught me to remember that the need to succeed affects oneself and those around that person. For me, it touched my children. The only thing I have ever wanted to do is make them proud of me. I never realized how my drive to achieve would cause them to feel that they were inadequate and needed to be perfect until my daughter told me she could not be as perfect as I was. She then listed the awards I had received. I was stunned. I told her I was far from perfect. And with the wisdom that belied her twelve years she looked at me and said, "You can rest now."

My presence will go with you, and I will give you rest.

—Exodus 33:14

Her words made me realize that my young daughter held as much insight about me as I did in my youth about my mother. This defining moment occurred when I heard her vocalize the same patterns of reasoning that led me to pursue perfection, altering my own perceptions of competition and ambition.

The fourth defining moment in my life is discussed in the epilogue of this book. This moment occurred when my mother passed away, when I began my process of forgiveness.

When I began writing this book about my mom, it was my way of learning more about who she was. As her daughter, I saw this gifted singer who stepped away from a successful career to become a mother. But as I read about Mom's career through newspaper clippings and her interviews, I learned that her choice to leave the world of show business was not her walking away from success, but a choice to move forward to another chapter in her life. That chapter was motherhood. Yes, her choice meant that I had become the center of her attention, and she was often my greatest critic. The life we shared was full of joy and pain, of loss and redemption. This woman who had no fear standing onstage in front of an audience of thousands withdrew to her home, fearful of going out in public. I watched alcoholism eventually claim her life, but despite the demons of her addictions, I knew that she loved me and made me feel safe when the future was uncertain for us.

In learning about my mom, I learned about who I was. I discovered that our mother-daughter relationship taught us how to be survivors. Mom showed me the power of faith. As her daughter, I have learned the healing power of forgiveness.

EPILOGUE

Faith and Forgiveness

When you hold resentment toward another, you are bound to that person or condition by an emotional link that is stronger than steel. Forgiveness is the only way to dissolve that link and get free.

—Catherine Ponder

EPILOGUE

The same thing that floods our heart and poisons our mind—the thing that has destroyed nations, businesses, families, and ultimately our inner being—is lack of forgiveness. My journey to reach this understanding was long. My youth was spent trying to destroy who I was because I didn't truly understand the pain I was feeling. As a young adult, I tried to cover up that pain. Now, as a middle-aged woman, I have discovered forgiveness and its power to set me free. If I do nothing else in my life, the one thing that is truly important to me is helping others understand what a life is like without harboring anger and hurt that stems from being unable to forgive. I know this book is about my journey to forgive my mother and ultimately myself. Yours may be to forgive a sister, brother, coworker, friend, or spouse. The who and the why don't matter; it only matters that you *do*.

Forgiving my mother came when I researched her life. It led me to an understanding of who she was and to recognize that she was still a child of God. Even if I felt jilted as a child, she was still a loved child of God. Even though I was angry at her actions, she was still a child of God. He loves her just as He loves you and me. Forgiving her was the most freeing moment I have ever experienced. As I sat going through those boxes my dad had sent to me after she died, I was able to see my mother through the eyes of others. With each new picture came new tears and healing forgiveness. Turning the negative over and finding the positive was something I had tried to do my entire life, but for some reason I had a hard time doing it in this situation. I believe that it was because I couldn't see past the unforgiving.

Without that forgiveness, I would have held on to the anger and hurt for the rest of my life. I can honestly say that once that wound became a scar, I grew exponentially as a person.

Forgiveness can bring great renewal. It can be a release from the bonds of the past—whether we forgive ourselves or forgive others.

As I tried to work through my anger alone I soon realized that I needed a little help. Like most, I turned to the internet to see if I could find information that would help me make sense of the emotions that had seemed to spiral somewhat out of control. That's when I ran across information about Dr. Luskin, who holds a PhD in counseling and health psychology from Stanford University. His research suggests that forgiveness can be learned. He did research involving families in Northern Ireland who experienced the death of loved ones due to the conflicts during "The Troubles." He found that people who are taught how to forgive become more optimistic and more forgiving in a variety of situations and more compassionate and self-confident.

All in all, I did learn to let go and look at things in a different light. If you learn to look at the people who hurt you through different glasses, it makes it easier to see their pain as well. I now ask the question, *why do they act the way that they do? Why do they lash out?* Almost always, I can look past the anger and find the hurt. I often feel sorry for them and then forgive them from a caring heart, not one that just sees the wrong-doing. It is a learned process that takes practice, but it is so worth the effort. I am so much more at peace.

When someone you love hurts you, you can hold on to the anger, resentment and thoughts of revenge—or embrace forgiveness and move forward to a more peaceful life.

—Dr. Fred Luskin

Forgiveness doesn't mean that one must deny another person's responsibility for causing hurt, and it doesn't minimize or justify wrongdoing. One can forgive people without excusing their actions. Forgiveness brings a kind of peace that helps everyone move forward with a fulfilling life. If you spend your time reliving the actions of people who caused you pain, you are choosing to spend time allowing them to hurt you all over again. But if you choose to forgive that person and move forward, you can spend time and energy on positive thoughts and actions. That in turn will improve your mood, thus improving your overall mind set and the outcome of your day.

We know that God is all-powerful. We also know that our prayers are answered in accordance with the One who loves us. There is a reason we are taught to forgive throughout the Bible. The Mayo Clinic cites a study about the effects of forgiveness on the body, which include sleep deprivation, increased risk of health problems, and early death. I wasn't shocked to find that some form of the word "forgive" was mentioned 116 times in the Bible (King James Version). Forgiveness is like food for the body that is necessary to stay healthy. The inability to forgive binds people, keeping them in a stranglehold. Grudges remain like wounds that fester, eventually hardening the heart to new experiences. Give it to God and see how much freedom comes back around.

Peace I leave with you; my peace I give you. I do not give to you as the world gives. Do not let your hearts be troubled and do not be afraid.

—John 14:27

CPSIA information can be obtained
at www.ICGtesting.com
Printed in the USA
BVHW03s0851120718
521082BV00005B/63/P